THE BLACK WIDOW

A collection of poetry inspired by true crime and
literary heroines.

LOUISE WORTHINGTON

Almost two-thirds of women in U.K. prisons are reported to be survivors of domestic abuse.

Contents

Black's Web   2

Key   6

Nemesis=Child   8

Toxic Love   9

One for Sorrow – Angela Cannings   11

Meadow's Law – Sally Clark   13

Packing   14

Safehouse   15

The Foster Mother to Claire Marshall's Traumatized

Children   17

The Interview After Leaving   20

Miniature Steps   21

Hieroglyphics   22

Common   24

Not Innocent Enough – Donna Anthony   25

Copper Wire   26

Lady Macbeth's Monster   28

My Last Duke   29

Stay Dead   30

Remembering the Dead   34

Mother Earth 37

White on Red 38

The House Misses You 40

Slow Deaths — Mary Ann Cotton 41

Poppy 43

Dear Birth Mother 45

His Rage 49

Drinks Like a Fish 51

Cause of Death: Self-Preservation 54

Anxiety 55

Walk Free 56

Black 58

Destructive Desire — Madame Bovary 59

They Send Her Back 61

Ghost Breath 64

Bound 66

Memory Binds 67

Birthmark 68

Beauty 69

Luke, My Evacuee 71

Survival of an Empath 74

Sally Challen 76

Lockdown; Skilled in Silence 78

A Smile   81

Loss   83

Fable   87

Counting Numbers – Trupti Patel   89

Bertha Mason   91

Museum Domes   92

Gift   93

About the Author   viii

By the Author   ix

Acknowledgements   x

Appendix   xi

Further Information   xviii

Dedication

To women and children in the past and in the present; to those whose voices were not heard and those who could not speak. To all my sisters.

Black's Web

The approach of evening throws the day's mysteries

Into more shadow.

Summer almost over,

Petals fall piecemeal,

A spectral drift of flowers.

A pink petal falls into a spider's web,

Nestles beside the mummified blackberries,

The ancient blueberries,

Together monstrous decibels of the dead,

Immortality on display,

Calling on the line, yet

When the breeze blows

Lace curtains quiver the dead.

From one side they catch the light and pulse,

Kid it isn't over,

But I know where age spots riddle my skin,

Where lines crosshatch my face.

I shall not make a shrine of this short life;

I shall not dwell on what was not or could/should

have been

Nor linger over what was, what is, what might…

No, the sky is flowering violets, roses, irises,

In mourning to this day.

Fever stains the clouds.

Devil's breath yawns across the landscape

A carnivore's smile —

For all the fiery hues, the heat has gone.

Cold hours ahead, and

The wind moans its age to remind us

Sleep is death's cousin,

Snaring until the sun shall rise again —

A second chance.

Moonlight, Black lures the bats

To circle on circles,

Spiral with the air —

"Come," Black calls. *"Come,*

Let's count the corpses hanging like stars.

See the silver moon through the windows of my
home,
Transparent tomb adored by the night.
Move, my sisters! Never be a still-life.
See the tiny wings fluttered by the breeze —
How the wind plucks their dead hearts,
Plays them a lyre string.
Watch the dead shackled in a silk hammock
As lips making silent prayers —
It is too late for them,
But not for you."

When the sun rises it christens Black's web
Guillotine,
But I say Teacher, with her landmark
Diagram.
I see a mural of tiny hearts suspended in time and
place,
Urging us to embrace
Loved ones, run to safety
Before we all reach
A sticky, Black end.

I see a bust

Framed by silk drapes

On stage: Black's Desire.

Her silk fingers beckon:

"Call by, play house, come see

The pictures hanging in my house.

Hunger makes us all companions."

As patient as a horse's graze

She signposts her desire to a mosaic,

This special way of being female;

Nothing is left to chance.

Her desire is precise, perfect as a papercut,

Mapped like the rings in a tree

Power line, to electrocute.

A breeze tugs at one of the victim's legs,

Toward a journey he cannot make.

A bundle caught fast,

Eaten slow.

Key

He says I am the keyhole, he the key,

Thinks I want him stuck into me. Thinks we slot

together,

Turn like clockwork hearts.

I know the door isn't locked.

I cannot open it. I'm shaking.

The door isn't locked.

London – there is no kind place to go;

I hear it's worse out there;

No one will believe me.

Who'd help me, a pisshead,

Penniless?

I'll try harder; he'll be nicer.

He loves me, really.

The death threats aren't so frequent

Now lockdown is over.

If I did call the police

They'd probably put me on hold,

Or put me through to non-emergency

Like last time.

He doesn't mean to make me bleed or break;

I bruise easily.

Tomorrow he will change; it will stop.

It's not like I'm mad, is it?

He's lovely when his mate's here.

It's all my fault; I deserve it:

I'm a useless cook/lover/cleaner/

person,

And he hates it when I choose my clothes/the meal/

drink/T.V. channel.

The door isn't locked.

I could leave if I wanted.

It's not like I'm trapped.

It's not like he's going to kill me.

Nemesis-Child

Giving birth to filth, to all the worst parts of myself.

Stitched my dirt together to make you,

Incubated, so my infection spread.

The malevolence soaked through into your genes,

Made your skin forever damp and seashell pink.

Out of a cobwebbed cave you came,

blackened and singed,

Every toe, finger, eyelash mine,

Expressionless, the facial features painted on,

Poisoned and friendless,

A tick on my blood.

Had I expected a serenade?

Soft touch, low voice to come out of me?

A gentle pulse?

A cat's tongue way of touching,

Decanting lies about loving me like holy water?

I have no desire to tame you.

You will bleed into the night and all the tomorrows

Long after I have gone to Hell.

Toxic Love

When I move
My bones scrape,
Full of him,
Fit to burst.
My abdomen is getting bigger and bigger;
I barely recognize myself.
Soon this satiated body
Will tear, a thin limb will protrude,
Perhaps try to escape to another host.
I hear it tapping against my sides,
Tapping, tapping,
Pushing, ripping, almost ripe,
Reminding me it's there —
As if I could forget.
I feel eyes explore my insides,
Tentacles entwined in my intestines,
Eating what I eat.
Hard to fully inflate my lungs

With Love there,

Growing,

Taking me over,

Becoming one.

A new day is born —

Love is out of my body,

But still the virus of desire and familiarity lingers.

The wound is infected, open.

Love's hand reaches down into my throat,

Bangs against the prison bars of my ribcage;

I hear it rip as Love crawls back inside

To undo me all over again.

One for Sorrow — Angela Cannings

Three young children stolen from the nest
By the magpie called Death.
One for sorrow,
Two were boys,
Three was a girl…

A second magpie called The Expert Witness spoke:
One cot death is a tragedy,
Two are suspicious,
Three are murder, until proven otherwise.
A third magpie stole Angela's freedom,
privacy, comfort, familiarity of fond places, of
treasured objects,
understanding about what happened: silence, love,
Inside her cell, with a pillow filled with magpies'
feathers.
A dove flew into the window and died;
The songbirds of Truth stopped singing for twenty

months.

Meadow's Law – Sally Clark

Sally's husband wasn't in the room

When their sons died – an omen was,

The darkest shadow of a cormorant

Squawking in the corner,

Sending Sally straight to Hell:

"And there's a 1:73 million chance

Of cot death happening to two children

In the same family" –

Not a wealthy, fancy family like this one.

One child dead after the other, less than two years

apart.

Packing

My suitcase is cracked open on the unmade bed.
I ransack our bedroom, rummage in the drawers.
Throw bracelets on like hoops at the fayre.
i grope in the dark wardrobe, finger clothes a
size/shade/style all wrong.
i pose in a pair of boots, a pair of mules.
The mirror lies:
There is nothing here of me. Nothing i recognize
of myself.
Have I already left?

Safehouse

The swan's nest of sticks,

Grebe's floating platform,

Egret's roost, high on a ledge,

The wren's soft-lined cup,

Leaves, grass, mould,

An entrance facing away

From cold winds,

The kingfisher's narrow secret tunnel,

The bald eagle's durable playpen,

Lined with feathers

Plucked from their breast,

The binding and waterproofing

from spiderwebs and lichens,

mud, saliva, caterpillar silk.

Structures of beauty,

Ingenuity,

Sacrifice,

Safety.

The Foster Mother to Claire Marshall's Traumatized Children

Sleep is a cage.

The Foster Mother holds her breath.

It's her spare room and she is afraid of being seen,

of looking, even.

Each panicked stare, each shuffling away

is a confession of failure,

of cowardice.

Relief:

She doesn't have to meet the children's fearful eyes

or reach out

To only be rejected.

Truth?

She cannot save them from their nightmares,

Cannot exorcize their past,

Poisoned by the violent death of their mother

By the man they knew as Father.

Witnesses in the living room,

The daughters watched the penknife hack at
mother's neck,
Then a larger knife to face, neck, head,
NECK.NECK.NECK.
There's no burial of childhood, of innocence,
No obituary,
No hymn,
No proof it is dead,
And yet
The iced breath of loss is here in this bedroom.
Why haven't all the petals fallen in the garden?
Lilacs in May, peonies in June, delphiniums in July —
They belong on their graves,
For these are not sleeping children,
But ghosts of their former selves.

The Foster Mother staggers onto the dimly lit
landing,
Closes her eyes on the sensations searing through
her:
A terrible birth of sorts, of understanding.
Barefoot on the plush carpet,

She pushes away the image of those black circles
under their eyes,
And closes the door on the bravest people she has
ever seen.

The Interview After Leaving

What are you made of?

Stories with happy endings,
Nursery rhymes sang in reverse,
Adventures on the moon and under the sea,
Pine trees in the earth,
Pine trees on a wagon,
Pine trees before cutting down to make a door.
I am made of the fallen autumn leaves.
I am the song of dawn in dew drops,
The tinkle of streams and tadpoles,
The running deer chasing its summer shadow,
The strength of storms and the muscle of the
imagination —
Anything but the burnt bacon smell of fear,
The rind of panic, the taste of hate.

Miniature Steps

A toothpick serves as a walking stick

To help me get out of bed.

This doll-sized house wants to eject me into the

world

Before I disappear,

For fear shrinks worlds to a pebble in a doll's pocket.

Dressed in clean clothes too big, too rough,

I open the giant front door

To walk on the moon.

Hieroglyphics

It's still a foreign feeling to have another person in
the house.

If Emma were a landlord she would evict this
tenant. This tenant, who smashes things, has no
regard for property, for people. For anything.
This tenant doesn't pay rent, or show love or
kindness to the landlady, lover, partner, friend.
They take, and there is a kind of homelessness about
the way they live. Squatting. A temporary effort at
each day, like it doesn't matter, like kicking
someone else's dropped litter.

Emma should stop glueing and sewing. Pretending.
This trail he leaves. The trail he steals.

The red felt-tip on the wall. The marks on her neck.
Not graffiti. Hieroglyphics.

Emma cleans, tidies away the broken things, fixes
what she can, puts hope into the electricity meter,
hoping to put warmth in her Pinocchio body, the
wooden hugs and Chinese Whisper lies. On the

worst days, she ties a ribbon on a pig and goes to the shops to buy all his favourite things.

Common

Michaelmas daisy are common in January,
Bouquets of red roses in February,
Bluebells in March and daffodils in April,
Apple blossom in May, Honeysuckle in June,
Lily of the Valley in July and cornflowers in August,
Sunflowers in September, delphiniums in October,
Carnations in November, poinsettias in December.

But domestic abuse is common all year round.

I leave this wreath to victims:
Black flowers for their secrets and blue forget-me-nots.
Strelitzia, the Bird of Paradise, for its promise,
Poppies for love,
A white Christmas rose for all the celebrations denied.

Not Innocent Enough – Donna Anthony

After six years in prison

You expect to be told

When to sleep and exercise,

When to wash,

What to eat.

You don't expect

To be trusted

With a knife to slice an orange.

It's the smell of the peeled orange

And its tangy zest

That reminds you you are believed.

A survivor called Donna,

An innocent, good woman

Who lost her two babies to cot death,

A rare bird who wasn't beaten by grief, injustice or

prison.

And there is a world beyond the cell,

Waiting for you to begin again.

Copper Wire

Yesterday and the days before that

he threw missiles at me,
made thunder on the landing,
rain=danced misery.
crisis was his element,
like copper wire conducting sparks.

but this day
he can't summon bats to the belfry of my mind.
his poison inside won't travel,
spit all he likes.
i am boarded=up windows,
a soft toy leeched of innards,
a landmark removed from the map,
a Degas dancer hanging on the wall in the finest
house,
as silent as a piece of cut hair falling to the floor.
i am all these things

because I am free.

Lady Macbeth's Monster

Loss stares at her all the while,

Watching her eat, sleep,

Tickles her earlobe with a rough smile,

Coos baby breath in too deep.

Nature's revolted, now chaos begs —

An empty womb worn for a face,

For nothing living can spawn from between her
legs,

Not even a blue skeleton in the finest lace.

Her belly now is coffin-flat,

Sharpened swords and daggers substituted for eggs.

Ambition multiplies like rats,

Drinks heartily between her damp, parted legs.

Motherhood, a miscarried dream,

Dead in the eye of a woman unseamed.

My Last Duke

A response to Robert Browning's dramatic monologue, "My Last Duchess".

There he is.

His gaze over my face like a fly

Inspecting its dead feast.

Now, with a finger

He traces the Cupid's arrow of my perfect lips

(painted a little too scarlet),

Like rain on a window —

Ah, the touch says treasure.

His epidermis smudges my glass casket.

It's tiring — the duke comes to visit again and again.

I am the flame —

I need no voice to make it known.

Look now, observe,

Burning bright, even in death,

And he the grey moth fading before my immortal

eyes.

Stay Dead

This night is afterbirth splayed up the walls of a
berth.
Anchor chains of my broken heart chink,
Plucking at the net curtain of my eyelashes,
A sick longing
'Til the scar of his voice speaks my name,
Exhales over the sound of salty waves,
Poking a paper-thin finger into a weeping wound,
Cleaning it with a dead tongue.

My body is a desolate ocean
Soon to be traversed —
No gentle voyage.
He smells of unspoken rituals.
Fear sits in my stomach like obsidian,
Rubbing 'til shards
Protrude as black icicles from my sternum.

"Clara, dear Clara,

Lower your eyelids on the night,
Undo the undoing –
I will make you still.
Let me embrace you tightly
So your chilled blood will turn to ice.
Let me in."

Splintering sound,
Oh, the dead wood of his voice:
A stark wooing,
A raven not a dove,
Settling like morning mist,
Cataracts in the eyes of a new lyric
Eyeballing the suffering of a haunted existence,
Tapping, tapping, scratching at the cabin door like a
cat's claws,
His pleas slip through the wooden cracks,
Wrap themselves on the ceiling
Between my breasts:

"Let me in, Clara.

Lower your eyelids.
There are new horizons with me.
Don't be afraid to be weak."

He feeds a sick hunger,
Navigates my loneliness,
Baits the salty air,
A presence of sour ambrosia,
Tickling emptiness,
Stroking desire for touch at this midnight hour,
A deathly rebirth to sleep with him.

I wish for the walls to flicker, the ceiling to fall and
show compassion.
His words are vines
Suspending my limbs from the ceiling,
Dressing the unmade bed in honeydew and lice.

"Surrender, dear Clara,
Let me stroke the trembling rhyme of your face;
Forbid I am ignored.
Heal the broken wings of your hips.

I'll send the sorrow away."

His eyes seek my flesh like a prayer and a sin,

A wedding of the rabid and unfed.

His spirit is my lover

Tonight,

Fat in my veins

Tapping on my skull,

Whispering in my ear.

The paralysis,

The numbness, is complete,

A perfect, glistening icicle.

The whitest flesh on the blackest of nights,

Into perilous gloom of no return,

From the clutch of his groping fingers

And melancholy pulse

Reborn —

Picasso's child in the shattered mirror of the sea.

Remembering the Dead

It is September 2022, England, and this elegy is incomplete.

Mariam Kamara, 46, was stabbed to death at home by her husband Amidu Komora.

Katy (Kathryn) Harris, 44, was murdered at home by her husband, Conrad Iyayi,

Yasmin Begum, 40, was stabbed to death in her home. Her estranged husband Quyum Miah was charged with her murder.

Ramona Stoia, 35, died from stab wounds to the neck. Police believe she was killed by her husband, who also killed himself. He had previously been questioned by police about sexually assaulting her.

Katie Kenyon, 33, was last seen alive getting into a vehicle in Burnley, Lancashire. Her ex-partner, Andrew Burfield, has been charged with her murder. At the time of writing her body has not been found.

Inayat Begum, 85, died at home with head, chest and abdominal injuries. Her son Mumtaz Ahmed has been charged with her murder.

Dolet Hill, 64...

Tanysha Ofori-Akuffo, 45...

Samantha Drummonds, 27...

Diana Gabaliene, 33...

Antonella Castelvedere, 52...

Margaret Una Noone, 77, was found dead by compression to the neck. Her son, Barry Noone, 45, has been charged with her murder.

Sakunthala Francis, 89, was stabbed to death. Her grandson, Verushan Manoharan, has been charged with her murder.

Wendy Morris, 76...

Abi Fisher, 29...

Hina Bashir, 21, was last seen alive and reported missing on 14th July. Her body was found in a suitcase on 17th July. Her boyfriend, Muhammad Arslan, 26, has been charged with her murder.

Samantha Murphy, 37...

Karen Dempsey, 55...

Margaret Griffiths, 87, died in hospital. Her son,

John Griffiths, has been charged with her murder.

Harleen Kaur Satpreet Gandhi, 32...

Hollie Thompson, 28...

Mother Earth

Come, Mother Earth,

Come,

Flood rivers,

Burst dams,

Wash away the crimson stains of pain,

Push out to sea the sinking boats of hopelessness,

Carry to shore the lifeboats of love and forgiveness,

Dry salty tears with the gentlest of light.

Come, Mother Earth,

Come,

Blow away the barricades of fear,

Dismantle the borders of self-doubt,

Rewrite the footprints in the sand,

Send them to the sand dunes,

To the sea grass,

To safety.

White On Red

The hulk is buried under a crumpled grey sheet.

A trembling wife opens the bedroom curtains

Onto egg-yolk light;

It runs onto the bedsheet,

Leached of colour, trying to escape from its

protective job.

A little finger protrudes as the tentacle of a great

grey slug

And a strand of black hair, like Bluebeard's whisker.

She cracks open the window

With more effort than it needs.

Breeze blows white kisses

From the bedside table;

The venomous powder he loves –

Those drifting fine particles – are forever

In the air between them,

A white out to a blood-soaked relationship.

Now she understands why he isn't stirring –

And never will hit again —

And the relief comes as quiet as falling snow,

As sure as a white leopard's footprint.

The House Misses You

A wire sculpture of hangers possesses the empty half of the wardrobe. Its doors have been slapped. The duvet is swollen, crumpled from the bags you hastily packed on the bed. Dust will find a forever home on your bedside table.

The sound of your laughter took flight a while ago, a paper plane on the trajectory of summer air. Now it is autumn, and the unflinching mirror in the hall won't retain your damaged look a second longer. Those limp curtains at the bay window can hang all they want in front of stretched raindrops.

Pillows have a memory of a foreign shape.

The cutlery is in the drawer but there's no hunger any more. All this, as the open fire cradles a scorched message in its hearth.

The house speaks.

Goodbye.

Slow Deaths – Mary Ann Cotton

Fallen.

Not like a shooting star

Or a loose garment, a seed or a tired leaf.

Not like a running child falling so far.

They bleed from the inside,

Not like a ripe apple from a single tree.

Fallen.

Fallen like the Cotton family tree,

The branches of three husbands, mother, eleven

children,

Doubled-up, bent in two,

Poisoned and spinning with pain.

Fallen like helpless flies into a web

Suffocated in silk and wed

With a venomous bite –

A forever goodnight

From Mary Ann Cotton,

A woman not broken.

Fallen.

Fallen with eyes wide open,

'Til justice came with a lasso

And slowly Black fell to Hell.

Poppy

Poppy dressed in a new school uniform,
Smelling strangely of lavender.
Night-time was free from sirens and shouts;
She didn't sleep.
Lotus petals
Had no meaning in her universe.

Bright white teeth of a stranger's sympathetic smile,
Father's cauldron of love,
The screams and cries pinning the day
To a blemished bedroom wall, that she understood,
Not the punishment of gentle cruelty.

Celebrities' children bear names
In memory of where they were conceived:
Paris, Chicago, Brooklyn.
When Poppy asked why her mother named her so
We could conjure fields of wild poppies,

Paint-red-spotted meadows,

Pretend she is as delicate and pretty,

But this child knows more

About the colour red

Than she should — a child

Steeped in her mother's blood

When she entered the world,

And every day since.

Dear Birth Mother

Dear Birth Mother

It seems I have the night shift. The grave-yard shift.
I must write about the jolly the superfluous the
banal the smiling face of the coin the side of the
pillow that isn't wet or hammered with nightmares
the good days the celebratory days like birthdays,
Christmas, tooth fairy nights.
So I won't tell you about wet Wednesday school
days, or too long summer holidays when we have
run out of things to do, or the sad days when she
won't tell me what's wrong, or the nights she can't
get to sleep, or the school days she falls out with her
friends and hangs around the monkey bars alone, or
the days she is distant from us we wonder if we
should touch her in case she breaks or the struggles
at school because of the endless hangover you gave
her.
Because I can't yet feel compassion for your loss and

I should be grateful for the gift of your daughter in our lives, but I am not, but I am but I wonder if you stare at the wall, at the place a picture used to hang and now stare at the nail in the wall? Whether your reflection bothers you? Or not at all.

I can't tell you that sometimes the moon drops too sharply for Libby, she doesn't know the family of stars or where she fits in the galaxy, trapped suspended in space and sky as a mobile above a cot where she once cried for hour after hour. How could you?

I could tell you about the nights I watch her sleep, her delicate eye-lashes, how I am amazed at the sleeping innocence of a child so severely treated who is brave enough to trust again and close her eyes on the dark, on a new home, a new family, and embrace it with what she has, how I am amazed at how far she has travelled and will travel, how her nerve memory is healing but still I see her clench her teeth when we touch her when it isn't on her terms and how a holiday is exactly the opposite of that.

~~I could tell you she is tethered here: we keep her safe, and we love her, but you know that. What you don't know is she locks the front door before she goes to bed, checks, checks again; when anxiety will grip her from nowhere, for no reason she can understand- but I do, you do. You made her vulnerable, and that gives Martin and I the night sweats. Not that you'd care. Sometimes her sadness is quiet as a fawn, gentle and shy; it seeks shade and secrecy; it watches all the time; other times, it booms, howls, leaves hoof-prints on the walls. She'll never be as good as new because of you, and you have given birth to a gorgeous girl, talented, strong and brave. A bull in a daisy chain. Heavy-footed, an earthquake of footsteps. Should she come to find you one day, you'll hear her coming like thunder. I hope she doesn't come looking.~~

Libby is sporty and full of fun like she cycled seven miles last weekend and played the part of pippi longstocking and on stage her face glows. She likes pop music, and she has a lovely singing voice like this year's winner on The Voice.

Her favourite meal is microwave pizza, followed by doughnuts with pink ice cream and apple juice.

Now she is nine she takes pride in brushing her long hair, which she wears in a ponytail for school and she can swim twenty-five metres and isn't afraid of the deep end like Martin is.

For Xmas we bought her a new bike, pink trainers she chose herself and the harry potter series which Martin and her take turns in reading. Libby wrote a long letter to Santa, and he left her a special pen and a diary which she writes in most nights before going to sleep. Libby writes better than me. Maybe better than you? We wouldn't know.

Did you get my last few letters? Libby would be happy if you bothered to write back. Hope your keeping well and all that.

Bestest,

Martin & Emma

His Rage

The walls of this kitchen turn pale,

Lean inwards and tremble.

Air, like the stress from his working day, aborts.

The wallpaper peels and bunches as a dog's rough

skin.

While my shadow is flattened against the wall,

The drawn blind on the dark sky

Has bolted open;

The window is a wide, unblinking eye

Frozen in fright,

Peering inside and outside onto darkness.

The house lights are on,

Stark,

Truthful.

Home is a mirage;

Echoes of his raw shouts have frosted the glass

windows,

Clouded the lightbulbs with red mist,

Dust from the floor has lined my lungs.

His dinner plate and mug are in the washing-up bowl

In pieces —

I carefully carry them to the bin in my shaking palm.

My skin is not thick enough for this.

Drinks Like a Fish

He has a recycling bin full of glass bottles to
remember her by.

On the anniversary of her death, he opens the lid
and sniffs to recall her morning breath, then tosses
in a daisy.

She left few traces in his house: High heels and spilt
blood made subtle marks in the carpet. The angle of
her hand on a wine glass sticks in his memory as a
splinter.

It could have gone on, except she forgot who he
was.

Still the kitchen remembers the cork's energetic
pop-slurred song. He'd told her if she carried on she
wouldn't reach thirty.

"There's worse ways to go," she said.

It could have gone on, except she forgot who he was.

As if from a tower of Shallot, she said she liked the view best through a wine glass: No edges or corners, softer shadows.
At first, he wanted to be the sugary liquid to coat her mouth, her pink insides. Then he wanted to burble and stew in her stomach, wanted to bend her lips out of shape, make her eyes blur, make her see him as he is...

It could have gone on, except she forgot who he was.

So, together they swam under a drunken moon. Her long hair tussled from the wet and the wind wound itself around her fair neck as she sang to the stars. The green sea turned her blue;
On the bottom of the ocean floor, there she lay, anchored by glass bottles. A fairy-tale ending for a drunken mermaid.

It could have gone on, except she forgot who she was.

Cause of Death: Self-Preservation

The curtains are parted. It is naked black in the bedroom, except for a slice of light exposing one hazel eye, the outline of his angular face. Clare knows how soft that eyebrow is to the touch, and how it is to be in the centre of that dark gaze.

Moving to the window, she peers outside. They will never be two names chiselled into a hill, hewn into rock. For months she wished she was that whisper of sunlight on his face. That and no more. The monster could be so gentle. He could.

The sirens sound. The sky is blue and white. White and blue. Colours of confession.

"I'm sorry I had to kill you," she says, knowing his death certificate will say "victim" – will say "murder".

Anxiety

No one can hear the bees but me. A cloud of hot voices gasp for air because they are maddened by containment in my brain, fed on sticky, undigested matter. A tyranny of half-formed slaves to distorted thinking, marinated in isolation. Together, the bees are a roaring disharmony, swarming mass, intense and incensed, glueing me to the armchair, where I long for a honey lullaby to put them to sleep, to let me be.

Walk Free

Who walks free

After the prison door is unlocked and opened,

when the shadows follow along the pavement

through your front door,

to dim every room in the house?

How do you grieve for the person you were

Before?

Yes, we know how time can slip away,

To forget incidentals,

But to have time stolen,

To have months, years, burgled

And never returned,

Compensated

By wrinkles, sleepless nights, the gravestones of

loved ones,

Shakes so bad you hold a mug of tea with both

hands,

And still it spills onto your lap?

By money that is never enough

Because it cannot undo time,

Buy time

Or love

Or forgiveness

Or health;

It cannot bring back who you were

Or change who you have become?

Black

Protected by instinct, not society's law

Fluent in chess

The fingerprint of silk

Elaborate halls and bedrooms

Silver walls

Keeping out Hell

Or keeping it in

An immutable world

Versed in the language of survival

Playing God like the law

Womanhood leaves no choice

No rations to her silence

Tumour of her bleeding aura

A black army of admirers

Fallen like stars cast from a false heaven

A close-up of the harshness of existence

Her Velcro touch is without fury

Our fittest survivor

Destructive Desire — Madame Bovary

It is difficult to get what you want

Wearing a pastel silk dress,

Straddling a man

Or climbing a ladder.

My desire made a salacious headline

For the myopic.

Look into these truffle eyes,

Tell me you don't feel the darkest of desires,

The swelling, the need; it cannot be healed —

Shamed, yes.

Because I am a creature of no authority;

I am living for myself.

I don't need to please you.

Are men terrified of me?

Condemn all you like,

Your approval means nothing to me.

There is no darkness in my mind or body.

Desire, you fools —

You cannot cut it out without killing me
And making you a murderer.
I possess my body;
You may borrow it only.
You are free to leave my side
Or stay.
I prefer to bite my tongue to make it bleed
Than do or feel nothing.

They Send Her Back

The tectonics of compassion move me to tears
sometimes.
Precious arrives in wind and rain with no coat.
Her eyes like blue cheese, runny above a short skirt.
No tights.
A look of tinfoil between her teeth.
Her knees look too big for those insect legs.
The knee joint hints at the baby fat she had
Once...
   rosy, full-fat cheeks
     plump innards
       smelling of apples
         An innocent gaze
Lost on *that day*
She's trying to forget,
When the ambulance came to take Mummy away
And she came to stay with me.

She moves slowly. Unpacks slowly. She fills only
one drawer of three, with dirty knickers curled up
into a ball of cardboard. A single white t-shirt laid
flat like a brocade to the filth beneath. Precious has
a permanent look of tiptoeing up threadbare stairs
too late to bed.
Before bed, I insist she takes a bath. Her feet turn
the water muddy brown. Having worn shoes two
sizes too small, the blisters on her toes and heels
anger me —

Like the dirty knickers, the dirty hair, the nest of
odd socks,
The smell of grease, the whiff of concrete and
tarmac and the barbed angles of her face hint at
trauma.

Piece by piece, as the days wane to weeks and
months, the sandbags diminish and the barricade of
fake smiles
Soften into sunlight.
She jumps at the foreign sound of carefree laughter,

Stops holding a pose, loses herself feeding the birds.
The splinters of her life
Soften, start to protrude;
We tug them out.

Tomorrow it is time for her to leave, to return
"home" to the people she calls family. I will water
the garden and, as the sunlight packs its bags, I
hope her face won't forget how a smile feels —
Remember how a laugh doesn't need to be followed
by a guilty look,
Like she's smashed an ornament.

Luke, My Evacuee

Luke's daddy left something for him to remember
him by:
A knuckle-shaped bruise, a dark purple nugget.
Syllables in deep hues
The strained vowels of truth:
"I hurt; you will, too."

Luke refuses to talk about it. Clutching a toy car, he
slides from view, sinking to the ground like a leaf in
Autumn. He remembers the sounds of impact,
flinches when the door closes.
When a sparrow flies into the window he ducks and
covers his ears, as though WWIII is here.
Perhaps it is, my little evacuee, shaking under the
kitchen table like he has vertigo. Luke will never be
allowed back home —
Like a bomb was dropped on it
And all the familiar places
Exploded

To nothing.

His smallness makes a giant of the room. From his stunned expression, he could have flown into the window. I want to scoop him up, put him inside a shoe box and watch him 'til the morning comes and sunlight lifts his wings.

Bound

"I am abused partner, expectant mother. I am not dutybound. I deserve better! Release me. Let me go!""

Black wraps silk so the victim will serve her,
Swaddles, dresses layer upon layer,
Bundles robes,
Slowly,
Slowly mummifies alive,
See no wings of hope;
A fading view impaired by ensnarement
Is without the horizon.

Memory Binds

If her memory serves her right
They'd honeymooned in Cornwall,
Kissed as soulmates in the sea…

Is she a fool to be in a riptide?

In the weak kitchen light
Broken blue crockery is a dead albatross.
Tears drip into the washing-up bowl,
An ocean searching for a shore.

Birthmark

The cotton towel is dropped to the carpet,

A sudden unveiling,

A snip of the ribbon.

The country of her skin

Smells of the sea, of the salty wind.

Precious eyeballs her naked body in the mirror,

Runs her hands over the bee stings,

Cuffs a wrist like she's a tailor,

Inspects an elbow, a knee,

Smiles when she wriggles her toes —

"The bits from my mother."

A eulogy.

Then she hitch-hikes to her kicked ribs,

Where her dreams got bruised and broken,

Where the tenderest shoots were stamped on

And boiling water thrown at her shadow,

Trapped in her own skin.

The ribs will heal

But she has a birthmark.

Beauty

I miss the disc in my lower back, the cartilage in my left knee and the hair that sits in the plughole of my shower. To look at me, you'd think I didn't sleep a wink — frankly, some nights I don't. The lid over one eye has slipped like a tile from a roof I shall never fix. For all that, I have never loved myself more. Parts of me are missing, but by God he is not one of them.

Police made an average of 669 child protection referrals to social services every day in 2021, because of incidents of domestic abuse across England and Wales.

Ghost Breath

He lives like a squatter in my house.

Without long, fair strands of hair

On the cushions, I couldn't tell

He is my son.

He grows taller, feathered, wilder,

Me smaller, quieter,

A mouse to a hunter, slow-cooked.

Calls me pulp or flotsam,

Sick fortune-teller,

Scarecrow mind,

Store-worker stockpiling mistakes —

I've heard them all before

From his stepdad's mouth,

Bear the imprint of him on my cheek;

I turn the other one,

Swallow my tongue, but

I smell human disaster —

A step-daddy who taught him everything he knows

—

See a slow-moving car crash with a demon behind
the wheel,
Feel winter and summer in my pale nightdress when
he leaves the house
Carting attitude like a rifle.

He returns in the small hours,
Me stuck tap-dancing in a silent movie
While he shouts: "Fuck You!" —
Says it like the words are a succulent peach,
Sucked and swallowed every millimetre of flesh
Until there's just the stone left
And the peach juice on his unshaven chin,
Summoning obscenities like insects into the trap of
his mouth.
I think stones are sewn inside him.
He dishes out pain for love,
Like he's seen a fist do when a tongue isn't enough.
Did I make him this way?
His burning eyes make me remember a younger me,
One without a medicine cabinet of lint and

ointment.

My eyes are sore —

I tell my son it's from chopping onions.

When I die

Who will be his performing dolphin,

My son?

He is my ugly legacy, my ghost breath,

The sediment of a life,

A broken mirror,

His stepdad's apprentice.

Survival of an Empath

The voices around her shout their woes.

Her whole house

Quivers.

The walls begin to shake.

Melancholy breeze pries its fingertips

Under her bedroom window,

Gusts through the keyhole,

Whistles tunelessly under the door,

Taps with brittle branches at the glass

In a rhyme of chaos,

'Til Empath is shivering blue,

Choking on pain.

She buries herself under the duvet,

A white pillow over a hanging face,

Whiles away the sunny day in curlicues of shadow,

Until the articulation of winter's frost and drifting

mist

Settles on the bleached floorboards

And Empath can rise from her solitary bed,

Leave unsteady footprints through tears,

Weakened but alive.

Sally Challen

Captain said it's Tuesday so it must be Tuesday,

Though the presenter on the radio said it's

Wednesday.

Living in the hull of his ship

Hybris is our figurehead;

We have our own sun and moon.

He says it's where i belong.

i should pay more attention,

Be like Mermaid he is with right now.

i wonder what day it will be tomorrow

And the day after that.

There was a 33% rise in domestic violence reports under COVID-19 lockdown.

Lockdown; Skilled in Silence

That was the year —

Years? —

When it rained vinegar,

Front doors corroded shut,

Cotton curtains stayed drawn as the island shrank,

Clouds like pillows muffled screams.

Some tongues were cut out,

The phones stopped ringing,

Translucence was removed from the dictionary —

The markers of morning, afternoon, evening —

Stolen and sold on the black market.

Passports were burnt,

Motorways travelled an unreachable distance,

The only colour was blue

From a gas ring,

Children stopped sleeping,

Stopped dreaming of the sweet-store and the park;

They learnt the demeanour worn for funerals

Before their mother was dead;

Some wore her brushstrokes

Or dreamt of them,

Forgot how helium feels.

Sharp utensils in the kitchen,

Blunt objects in the garage

Stopped being dormant,

Grew eyes like dark sugar,

While some houses were wiped off the map.

Did rivers stop flowing?

The rushes bent down to listen

But the acoustic had gone.

Leaves were torn from trees

And no one noticed;

A motherless landscape.

There was no sound outside to celebrate a new day,

Not even from the lark.

How do we record in history

The sorrows kept out of sight?

How did the voices sound of the dead?

Perhaps we should plant bulbs in the earth:

Amaryllis with wide open mouths,

Cold weather lilies,

White and red roses in denizens of houses?

The light will find the way;

Let spring and summer come to their door.

Perhaps from their colony of homes

wallpaper should be stripped,

The lies laid bare:

Safe as houses.

Family.

The letters left for you and me:

Ranjit Gill, 43...

Helen Joy, 54...

Christina Arnold, 71...

If only a scraper was the answer

To show we really did care.

A Smile

Savour it

As a first day of spring,

The dapple of warm light on daffodils,

The delicate heads of snowdrops lifting a little,

The end of a monochrome horizon.

It feels like

A statue has moved.

When mothers are convicted, their children are often taken into care with foster carers or adopted. When a conviction is overturned, most children will remain in care.

Loss

You are seven

Separated from your mother for eleven days

You have searched the house

Opened every drawer and cupboard

Climbed the ladder into the loft

Thinking it was futile but doing it anyway

You have searched the garage

Looked in the car, even the boot

Then you search outside

A vast, untamed garden

Backing onto open fields

Rich with oilseed rape and wheat

The hedges are thick, the nettles wide

And grass knee high

Thick ferns to shoulder height

It seems now you have called Mummy so many

times

It should echo back in sympathy

Your voice is strangled as you call and call again

Missing, missing, not presumed dead, not presumed
dead

Still hope, a chance of finding her, making
everything right

Normal

You crawl on your hands and knees through the tall
grass

Peeking between stems like a cat hunting a mouse

Wet leggings from the earlier rain cling like a
second skin

You climb over the gate into the field

The oilseed rape is thick

You push hard to break through

Like breaking membranes

Your calls are desperate, throat parched

The urgency still there

But exhaustion is on the horizon

You are thirsty but unable to drink

Unable to do anything except search...

How can this have happened?

Why me?

Did I do something wrong?
You go back inside the house
To look again
Angry now, you smash an ornament
The making-happen feels good
For a second
Through the window
The fields of rape seed and wheat shiver in the
breeze
But you only see absence

You see Mummy everywhere
And nowhere
You see her name written on the grey sky
On the underbelly of gathering clouds
On the tips of wheat nodding so cheerfully
So perfectly
You keep looking, looking
A singular purpose
A desperate preoccupation
To find what you have lost

What you will never have

Will go on forever.

Fable

Black paints with the tiniest of brush strokes.

Brushes over winter hue with the lightest touch,

Where the post and rail fence meet the gatepost.

As a whisper of fingernails, he comes —

Ah, the rasp of his legs as he walks the fence,

The enticing knuckle of his insect body.

He abseils down the fence a fraction,

Guided by appetite,

Oblivious to the encore of mistakes.

Its empty torso swings to the target;

The stuntman falls as if into a broken net

Put into his place: *lie still.*

Like a black shoe

In mid-footfall,

Kicking its way between Heaven and Earth.

The afternoon throws shadows

As old medallions over the grass,

A still-life in waiting for the drapes of nightfall.

Sunset, the sky grows red and violent,

Straight from the butchers.

There, a sinister, smiling face with insects for eyes.

Rain falls and, wearing a veil of sadness,

The winds gust.

Black's fable remains to be read.

Counting Numbers – Trupti Patel

Baby Amar, Jamie, Mia,

why did you die before the season changed?

Mummy, your grandmother lost five in infancy –

How can this be so?

Shall we ask The Expert Witness again?

He believes in statistics, is good at maths because he

knows

There are twenty-four ribs in a ribcage

Be it child or adult,

And Mia's ribs were fractured:

1,2,3,4 . . .

And statistically cot death is ruled out:

1,2,3 . . .

Says cot death doesn't run in families:

1.

Says murder does and a fitting sentence is

∞

Can he accurately count the lives fractured by

injustice? Can he?

Bertha Mason

Metal chains clink as the dog —

A foul-smelling mongrel of a thing —

Strains toward the attic window.

It is summer and flies keep her open wounds

company.

Her head sways as she stands and staggers,

As her master refills the water bowl,

Thinking her a demented wolf,

Never knowing gentle touch

Or kind tones —

A life ensnared.

Knowing only the violent ways of a master,

She cowers in the shadows,

Watching with bloodshot eyes,

Baring her teeth and snarling,

Desperate to drink.

Not born this way...

Made.

Museum Domes

The survivor has to know their identity; they know
history can't be cut out, cured, transplanted,
however rotten.

She finds her pickle jar cloistered on a white shelf, a
dust-free specimen. Still-life, perfectly preserved in
formaldehyde. It's part of them, like a diseased
kidney, a drinker's liver.

The survivor smashes the museum dome, sending
shards of glass onto the kitchen floor and a vinegar
stench into the air.

In the explosion of sound and form, a beautiful,
unique creature emerges,

Her bones lovingly healed, scar tissue intact.

She loves the beautifully imperfect whole of herself,
A legacy of her braveness.

It's only natural she opens the window and lets the
bird fly into the room.

Gift

I spin silk thread

For the hurt and lonely,

For the sleepless and lost.

I spin for those who wear dark glasses in the rain,

For those who bruise at the memory of a voice.

I spin for those

Naked under their clothes,

For those whose heart beats

Like a spade on buried bones.

I spin for the eyes

That ache in the darkness.

I spin to make whole the fragments

To make an aperture

To move through,

From this to another just world,

A mouth to wish you

A happy day,

A good night's sleep,

Peace on Earth.

About the Author

Louise Worthington writes psychological fiction and dark poetry. She is the author of seven novels and two short story and poetry collections, and lives in Shropshire with her family. She is a member of the Horror Writers Association.

https://louiseworthington.co.uk

By the Author

Novels:

Forgotten Dark

Rosie Shadow

Doctor Glass

Rachel's Garden

The Entrepreneur

Willow Weeps

Distorted Days

Short stories and poetry:

Stained Glass Lives

Visited by Dreamscape

Acknowledgements

"They Send Her Back" — *Medusa Tales.*

"Survival of an Empath" — *Dark Winter Literary.*

"Ghost Breath" — *The Horror Zine,* Fall 2022.

"Stay Dead" — *The Horror Zine,* Fall 2022.

"Anxiety" — *Paragraph Planet.*

"Confession" — first appeared in a revised version in *Entropy.*

I would like to thank Joe Shooman for his thoughtful and subtle editing.

Appendix

Angela Cannings's daughter Gemma died from cot death, aged thirteen weeks. In April 2002, Angela was sentenced to life imprisonment for the murders of her two sons, Jason (seven weeks old) and Matthew (eighteen weeks old). She appealed this decision, and in 2004 was found to be the victim of a miscarriage of justice and released from prison.

Sally Clark was convicted of the murders of her sons, Harry, eight weeks old, and Christopher, eleven weeks old, in 1999. Her first appeal in 2000 was rejected, but it was recognized that the 73-million-to-one statistic was flawed. In 2003, her conviction was quashed after new evidence came to light.

"Meadow's Law" — the name is derived from the controversial British paediatrician Roy Meadow, who until 2003 was seen by many as "Britain's most eminent paediatrician" and leading expert on child abuse.

At the age of twenty-five, **Donna Anthony** was convicted of the double murder of her two babies, in 1998. She served six years in prison before her sentence was overturned on appeal.

"Lady Macbeth's Monster" is based on Shakespeare's tragedy *Macbeth* (1606), and Lady Macbeth's miscarriage. *http://shakespeare.mit.edu/*

"My Last Duke" was written in response to Robert Browning's poem, "My Last Duchess" (1842):

FERRARA

That's my last Duchess painted on the wall,
Looking as if she were alive. I call
That piece a wonder, now; Fra Pandolf's hands
Worked busily a day, and there she stands.
Will't please you sit and look at her? I said
"Fra Pandolf" by design, for never read

Strangers like you that pictured countenance,

The depth and passion of its earnest glance,

But to myself they turned (since none puts by

The curtain I have drawn for you, but I)

And seemed as they would ask me, if they durst,

How such a glance came there; so, not the first

Are you to turn and ask thus. Sir, 'twas not

Her husband's presence only, called that spot

Of joy into the Duchess' cheek; perhaps

Fra Pandolf chanced to say, "Her mantle laps

Over my lady's wrist too much," or "Paint

Must never hope to reproduce the faint

Half-flush that dies along her throat." Such stuff

Was courtesy, she thought, and cause enough

For calling up that spot of joy. She had

A heart—how shall I say?— too soon made glad,

Too easily impressed; she liked whate'er

She looked on, and her looks went everywhere.

Sir, 'twas all one! My favour at her breast,

The dropping of the daylight in the West,

The bough of cherries some officious fool

Broke in the orchard for her, the white mule

She rode with round the terrace—all and each

Would draw from her alike the approving speech,

Or blush, at least. She thanked men—good! But thanked

Somehow—I know not how—as if she ranked

My gift of a nine-hundred-years-old name

With anybody's gift. Who'd stoop to blame

This sort of trifling? Even had you skill

In speech—which I have not—to make your will

Quite clear to such an one, and say, "Just this

Or that in you disgusts me; here you miss,

Or there exceed the mark"—and if she let

Herself be lessoned so, nor plainly set

Her wits to yours, forsooth, and made excuse—

E'en then would be some stooping; and I choose

Never to stoop. Oh, sir, she smiled, no doubt,

Whene'er I passed her; but who passed without

Much the same smile? This grew; I gave commands;

Then all smiles stopped together. There she stands

As if alive. Will't please you rise? We'll meet

The company below, then. I repeat,

The Count your master's known munificence

Is ample warrant that no just pretense
Of mine for dowry will be disallowed;
Though his fair daughter's self, as I avowed
At starting, is my object. Nay, we'll go
Together down, sir. Notice Neptune, though,
Taming a sea-horse, thought a rarity,
Which Claus of Innsbruck cast in bronze for me!

The names in the poem **"Remembering the Dead"**
have been taken from
https://twitter.com/CountDeadWomen/status/15718
87593184235520 and https://kareningalasmith.com/.

Mary Ann Cotton, born on Halloween in 1832, is
thought to have poisoned three husbands, one lover,
her mother and eleven of her thirteen children with
arsenic. A slow, painful death was had by her victims
and herself, owing to a misjudgement by the
hangman.

"Dear Birth Mother" is based on the idea of "letterbox
contact", whereby carers communicate to birth

parents via social services.

"Destructive Desire" is based on the character of Madame Bovary, from the novel by the same name. *Madame Bovary* (1856) was written by Gustave Flaubert

Sally Challen murdered her husband of thirty-one years, Richard Challen, in 2010, with a hammer. They had two sons. She was sentenced to 22 years for murder, reduced to 14 years following appeals and new psychiatric evidence of coercive control.

Coercive control is a form of domestic abuse which is now a criminal offence. It is an act or a pattern of controlling behaviour, acts of assault, threats, humiliation and intimidation, depriving the victim of independence.

Trupti Patel was initially charged with three counts of murder. She was acquitted in 2003.

"Bertha" is based on the character from *Jane Eyre*

(1847) by Charlotte Bronte, who is emblematic of the "mad woman in the attic":

"In the deep shade, at the farther end of the room, a figure ran backwards and forwards. What it was, whether beast or human being, one could not, at first sight, tell: it grovelled, seemingly, on all fours; it snatched and growled like some strange wild animal, but it was covered with clothing, and a quantity of dark, grizzled hair, wild as a mane, hid its head and face."

"Ghost Breath" is based on the idea of the cycle of violence, otherwise known as the "intergenerational theory", when considering the effects of domestic abuse on children. However, research findings are inconsistent, and there is no automatic cause-and-effect relationship.

Further Information

https://www.nationaldahelpline.org.uk

https://www.womensaid.org.uk

https://www.justiceforwomen.org.uk

https://evidencebasedjustice.exeter.ac.uk

https://womeninprison.org.uk

https://www.ranker.com/list/10-ruthless-black-widow-killers-whose-crimes-made-history

https://www.legislation.gov.uk

https://www.nspcc.org.uk

https://www.whitehavennews.co.uk/news/17139465.brutal-killer-launches-high-court-appeal/

https://www.msichoices.org.uk/news/33-rise-in-domestic-violence-reports-under-covid-19-lockdown

https://twitter.com/CountDeadWomen/status/1571887593184235520

https://kareningalasmith.com/

If you are experiencing domestic abuse, you are not alone.

The National Domestic Abuse Helpline is a freephone, 24-hour helpline, which provides advice and support to women and can refer to emergency accommodation.

0808 2000 247.

Printed in Great Britain
by Amazon